T0169934

Honoring the Stones

Honoring the Stones

poems by
James O'Hern

CURBSTONE PRESS

FIRST EDITION, 2004
Copyright © 2004 James O'Hern
ALL RIGHTS RESERVED.

Printed in the United States on acid-free paper
Cover design: Stone Graphics
Cover photograph is of La Roche aux Fées, Ille-et-Vilaine, France.

NATIONAL
ENDOWMENT
FOR THE ARTS

This book was published with the support of
the Connecticut Commission on the Arts, the
National Endowment for the Arts, and
donations from many individuals. We are very
grateful for all of their support.

Connecticut Commission
on the Arts

Library of Congress Cataloging-in-Publication Data

O'Hern, James, 1933-
  Honoring the stones / by James O'Hern.
    p. cm.
  ISBN 1-931896-03-8 (pbk. : alk. paper)
  1. Stone—Poetry. 2. Nature—Poetry. 3. Mexican-American Border
Region—Poetry. I. Title.
  PS3615.H47H66 2004
  811'.6—dc22   2003027093

published by
  CURBSTONE PRESS   321 Jackson Street   Willimantic CT 06226
      phone: 860-423-5110   e-mail: info@curbstone.org
                www.curbstone.org

ACKNOWLEDGEMENTS

I would like to thank my teacher, Colette Inez, for her patience and loving support over these past six years and to acknowledge my indebtedness to Stellasue Lee whose friendship and encouragement have been vital to my poetry. I also wish to express my gratitude to Gloria Anzaldúa, Joy Harjo and Nuala Ní Dhomhnaill. These three poets, above all others, have served me as models for truth, the integrity of language, and commitment to the ancient tribal spirit.

Poems in this collection originally appeared in these publications whose editors I would like to thank:

Spillway: "A Hundred Words for Anger"

Rattle: "A Prize Watermelon"

"The Pond", "Chispa", and "Rock Soup" appeared in *13 Los Angeles Poets* edited by Jack Grapes, published by Bombshelter Press (1997).

Contents

THE SEARCH

For Muddy

HONORING THE STONES

THE BORDERLAND

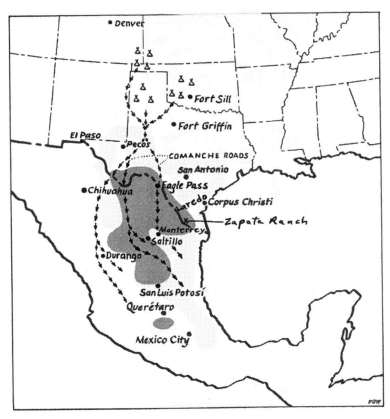

Source areas of peyote (shaded area) (after Anderson 1969) and
Comanche roads from the Southern Plains into Mexico, 1840-70 (after
Ralph A. Smith 1961).
Source: *Peyote Religion: A History* by Omer C Stewart. Copyright ©
1987 by the University of Oklahoma Press/ reprinted by permission.

The peyote area shown coincides with the natural range for growing mescal and both lie within the region of the Chihuahuan Desert which is bounded on the west by the Sierra Madre Occidental and on the east by the Sierra Madre Oriental. The desert extends as far south as the San Louis Potosi in Mexico and north into New Mexico and Arizona.

For at least 10,000 years this land has been considered sacred to aboriginal tribes that lived here. Some say the "Home of the First People" was lost somewhere in this desert as Atlantis was lost in the sea. Even today, members of the Native American Church conduct an annual pilgrimage to Mirando City, TX (30 miles from Laredo), and the Huichols walk north on a sacred journey from their homeland to a location near San Louis Potosi.

COMANCHE ROADS

Before I was born
before borders and barbed wire
Indians from the valleys of Mexico
followed herds of deer and buffalo
on migrations north into the Great Plains
and back again

Each year from Mexico
a band of devout Huichols
walks north for forty days
following tracks of sacred deer
along the foothills of Sierra Madre Occidental
And from the north
Cherokee, Shawnee, Tonkawa, Kiowa
Comanche, Choctaw, Chickasaw...
travel south on the *Old Comanche Roads*

Seeking the *Spirit Home of the First People*
hidden behind a place called *Clashing Clouds*
on the upper reaches of the Chihuahuan Desert
between   *Where the Vagina Is*
and   *Where the Penis Hangs*
in the land   *Where the Sun was Born*

TESTIMONY

like that bright day
four point nine million years ago
when the first of our fathers stood upright
and swaggered slowly across the savanna
trying to impress his mate-to-be
with the power of the first *full frontal*
like the day my father stepped out of the shower
cloaked in a cloud of steam
the glistening torso of a Roman soldier
a towel for a head, no arms, no feet
a weapon in the shape of a cross
dangling from his waist
as Adam in the Old Testament
I cupped my hands over my cluster
bearing witness in sacred testimony
to the Holy Trinity
and from that day understood
why my father sat for hours in the basement
working neat's-foot oil into the black
twelve foot long glistening body of the bullwhip
braiding white silk tips on the end
so the snap would sound like a gunshot

THE CRY

Sometimes in the crib
I dreamed my mother was dying
and woke with a cry in my throat

Sometimes the cry came from me
sometimes from her room
sometimes from the dark

If she was there in the morning
it was the coyotes calling
and I'd be fed to them in the night

One moonlit night they came
laughing and scratching at my screen
...like I was a dying rabbit

And before they left
pissed on the front porch
and called my mother's name

Los Danzantes
Bas-relief figure of a so-called Danzante or 'dancer';
a portrait of a slain enemy whose name glyph
appears in front of his mouth.

Source: *Mexico. From the Olmecs to the Aztecs*
By Michael D. Coe, Thames & Hudson, Ltd., London

MONTE ALBAN

A slain enemy
blood flows from his chest
with his last breath, he coughs out his name

I recognize something in him
the meaning will come
if I avert my eyes, show proper respect

and say the words as a Zapotec
Mixtitlan, ayautitilan
out of the clouds, out of the mist

In a dream, I am a were-jaguar
the infant with a cleft head
held dying in the lap of the fire god

Who is the enemy?
My father comes up from the cellar
breaking the door down with an axe

My mother takes me by the heels
wields me like a club
and bludgeons him to death

THE POND

By the end of summer
When the water in the pond
Turned black
It was my job to save the fish

At the edge of the pond
Dreaming of golden reefs
I heard the cry of tadpoles...
Tiny whales longing for the sea

I saw teeming histories
Castles and creatures of the deep
Stacked beneath the surface
Like generations of an ancient city

Water choked with algae
Drained away—
I embraced and bundled
Slimy stalks of drooping lilies

And chased fingerlings
From catchment to catchment
Scooping them into buckets
With a kitchen sieve

When the pond was safe again
Scrubbed clean in quicklime
By the gardener in rubber boots
I licked the trembling hearts

Of scum-covered minnows
Replacing them
One by one
Into the reborn waters

And said a child's prayer
Hoping that one day
When my sky goes black
One of them will remember

LA ALBERCA

Al fin del verano
cuando el agua en la alberca
se ennegrecía
era mi tarea lavar a los peces

Al lado de la alberca
soñando de arrecifes dorados
escuche el grito de los renacuajos
pequeñas ballenas anhelando el mar

Vi historias repletas
castillos y criaturas de mar profundo
amontonados como generaciones
de un ciudad antigua

Vaciamos el agua
atascada de algas
y abracé y envolví
los tallos viscos de nenúfares caídos

Persiguiendo a los pececillos
de charco a charco
cuchareándolos en baldes
con un cedazo

Cuando la alberca ya estaba limpia
bien fregada con cal viva
por el jardinero con botas de goma
Lamí los corazones temblorosos

De los pececillos cubiertos de verdín
devolviendolos
uno por uno
a las aguas renacidas

Y dije una oración de niño
rogando que un día
cuando mi cielo se ennegrezca
uno de ellos me recuerde

TEXMEX HISTORY

My mother would say—
"You are pure Irish and don't you forget
  who you are or where you came from"
but I didn't feel Irish
and wasn't sure about being Texan
having grown up on the border
where most of the Texans I knew
were Mexicans
and it wasn't such a good idea
to be Mexican
unless you lived in Mexico
and Mexicans in Mexico
wanted to be Spanish
            where ladies of rank
            had dark fuzz above the lip
            and didn't shave their legs

and you wouldn't want to be Mestizo
worse to be pure Indian
with an Oriental look about the eyes
and a back-slanted forehead

CHOCOLATE

The desert a giant stone mortar
ground everything down into candy
leche quemada a poor man's chocolate
made from burnt milk and *carrizo*
candy darker and richer going south
from *leche quemada* to *chocolate*
chocolate chocolatl xocolatl
past mountains and cities
a smoldering pot of dark red *chili mole*
where the bowels of earth boiled over
30000 years ago at the volcano of Xcitli
leaving a thick dark crust of ashes and blood

Where everyone ate earth with one finger
upon arriving at a new place
made offerings of flowers and fire
burning incense of *copali*
in rattle-stone ladles made of clay

Where men slashed their ear lobes in prayer
drank *chocolate* with ground up flowers
chocolate with *chilis* and *octili* wine
with cakes of waterfly worms
and sang this song before the deity
attesting to the purity of heart

> *yc nima tlalquia*
> *y aquin ynic quineltliaia*
> *itlatol*[1]

---

1. *If what you say is true, eat earth*

14

XOCOLATL

El desierto es un molcajete gigante
que mole todo al caramelo
cambiándolo a chocolate de los pobres
con leche quemada y carrizo
un dulce más oscuro y rico
cuando más se va al sur
de leche quemada a chocolate
chocolate *chocolatl xocolatl*
allende las montañas y ciudades
olla hirviente con chili mole oscuro
donde las entrañas de la tierra rebosaron
30000 años atrás en el volcán de Xictli
dejando espesa corteza de cenizas y sangre

Al llegar a un lugar nuevo
comían la tierra con un dedo
haciendo ofertas de flores y fuego
quemando incienso de *copali*
en un cucharon y troqueta de barro

Donde los hombres cuchillaban
el lóbulo de las oreja bebiendo
chocolate con flores molidas
chocolate con chilis y *vino vctili*
comiendo *tecuitlatl y vcuiltamali*
cantando esta canción para su dioses
testigando a la pureza del corazón

> yc nima tlalquia
> y aquin ynic quineltliana
> *itlatol*[2]

2. *Si lo que dice es la verdad, come la tierra*

CÁNTAROS
(jugs that sing)

Aunt Ada big as a *casa* lived in Mexico
in the village of Tepeyacac
where she crawled on her knees
to take communion
at the altar of the Black Virgin
Our Lady of Guadalupe
descended from Tonantzin (blood eater)
mother of Quetzalcoatl and Tezatlipoca
Gods known to me
from the cardboard copy of the codex
Aunt Ada gave me for my 6th birthday

Her tiny house crammed full of trinkets
Huichol masks with human hair and teeth
tarnished silver tree of life on the wall
a small *cántaro* from Tonala
made of *barro canelo* an aromatic clay
women of the day chewed to get high

She poured water into the *cántaro*
filling the room with the scent of flowers
but didn't let me drink from it
said it makes little boys *loco*
took me on her lap to tell me
the Aztec version of Christ on the cross
how flowers spilled from the wound
when His body was pierced

Before God gave us His Only Begotten Son
before the first Seven Days of the Holy Bible
giant green bats drank the blood of children
and shat the world into existence

If you listen at night
you still hear the cries of children
as giant bats nibble their toes
in the caves of Sierra Guadalupe
where cannibals still hunger
and bats hang their heads in shame

My Aunt Ada comes to me in a dream
I am perched on her lap
afraid I will fall in when she laughs
she hands me the *cantaro*

I drink from it
taste the earth that sings—
      Take eat...His body and blood
      which was given for thee...

Ke-e-eala, ke-e-eala, isoe-e-eiala, wando
wisloe esaeilala
ke-keala oae-e-eao.[3]

---

3. This is a song they say an old woman recited in a
sacred language and that is why we cannot explain it.
The elders say it refers to all the suffering the earth
was to endure in this world. (p.76, *The Mythology of
Mexico and Central America* by John Bierhorst)

Ceramic plate with two rabbits, painted by Amado Galvan, 1940.

Source: *Nagual in the Garden: Fantastic Animals in Mexican Ceramics*,
by Leonore Hoag Mulryan;
UCLA Fowler Museum of Cultural History.

CHISPA

On days he fixed a stew
cooking it down to a hot red oily stock
added hominy, vegetables, salt pork
bits of meat from a rabbit he shot
served it with tortillas de harina
chili piquines that raised a blister
if the juice touched your lip

In the shade of the lean-to
we watched *plumas de fuego*
"feathers of fire" flutter on end
drain color from the underside
of fresh turned clods of gingerbread earth
and below the fields, the Rio Grande
laid out along the flat river bed
like the molted skin of a rattlesnake

as Chispa began to chant
Ay ya yao
ayya yya ynye au
coztic quauhtli, coztic coyotl
coztic coatl, coztic tochin, coztic macatl

A Nahuatl song of animal dreams
how to get inside their skin
sueños de nagual about a yellow eagle,
yellow coyote, yellow snake, yellow rabbit,
yellow deer

He taught me to call quail
blowing ocarina notes
through my thumb knuckles
to call up rutting bucks

with a doe's wail bleated out
on a mesquite carved cacto-reed

In the rabbit's dream
I become the prey—
from the edge of a child's voice
give the high pitched scream
of a dying rabbit

When the rabbit is caught
in the jaws of the coyote
it sings three songs

A cry of alarm
warning others not to come
When fangs crack his skull
a shriek of terror shatters the dream
The last notes are the weeping of a child

Chispa sings
Ay ya yao
ayya yya ynye au
yyaha, yya yya, yya ayya, ayyo oviya
temictli, quitemiquiz, tochtiz[4]

Crouched behind a clump of mesquite
I finish the song and look up
into the snout-sharp glare of a she-coyote
locked eye-to-eye with me as rabbit
her four running mates frozen still

None of us know what comes next
until she breaks the spell

4. *Dreams, he will dream of it, he will become a rabbit.*

acknowledging me as if to speak
As she turned to leave
I swear—I heard her laugh

Yyaha, yya yya, yya ayya, ayyo oviya
ayya yya, ayya yya yyo viya, ayya yya ayya
yya
yyo viya

So goes the rabbit's song

ROCK SOUP

Chispa puts a rusty iron pot on the wood stove, stokes it with mesquite and begins making soup. He pours water from a clay jug balanced on his hip, adds greens, onions, peppers and fresh tomatoes I brought from the market. Turnips and long white radishes came from his garden patch out back. He takes out an old wooden box lined with parchment and pinches out a palm of red dirt, asks me to taste it and put some in the pot. It is magic clay for rock soup, he says.

While the pot boils, we go outside to the shade of a lean-to looking out over the shimmer of glazed dirt fields to the river below. Where we planted cedar fence posts until my hands bled, strung barbed wire as tight as a piano.

There is a time in the Mexican desert
when nothing moves
No living thing quivers, twitches or crawls
not even to save itself

The sun arcs to its peak
rivers run onto themselves as they slow
making big loops in the mud
and shadows blur under the scrub

Chispa gets up, motions it's time to start the hunt. Bare to the waist and without guns, we begin. First the creek beds. Scanning under scrub brush, squinting for shadows that shouldn't be there, we study rocks looking for an eye blink. Suddenly, Chispa leaps up. Both of us hurdle full speed over brush chasing the cottontail flushed out, not from behind a rock but, the rock itself bounding away and we follow side-stepping, vaulting over and through, jerk to a halt when the rabbit slows...then go again, flushing the rabbit to the next spot—seven times: the running, flushing, stopping—until finally the rabbit stops under a scrub—gasping, gagging—shows us a tiny pink tongue. Chispa walks over and gently picks him up by the ears.

He hands me the rabbit to carry back to the shack. Cradled and quiet in my arms, his heart whirs against my chest. Inside, Chispa lifts the rabbit by the ears again, stretching him lengthwise over the pot as I hold his body. Then he slits the rabbit's throat letting hot blood pour out into our soup.

When we finish lunch, we take a nap in the shade of the lean-to. I close my eyes to the sound of chanting. Chispa says he's offering a prayer of thanks to the rabbit in its own tongue.

PRIZE WATERMELON

I carry a huge striped watermelon
cradled in my arms like a baby
making my way slowly
across deep rows of a plowed field
toward the blue '38 Ford pickup

Chispa stands in the truck bed
in white chinos, sweat-stained Panama
knee-deep in watermelons
arranging them so they won't break
on the bumpy ride back

I lift my prize to him
it bumps off the running board
onto hard ground and splits open
exposing that I am not yet a man
big enough to help

Chispa taught me *la vida es un sueño*
life is a waking dream
seen through the eyes of a *nagual*[5]
he asks *¿que quiere decir el sueño?*
I answer it is a bad omen
that my life is a failure
I cannot do anything right
and he says, *ahorita, dame un pedacito*

I hand him a piece
he motions for me take one
as we eat the hot sweetness

5. Nagual: *a fantastic animal, spiritual double.* Nahui olin
in Nahuatl means "movement of the heart".

asks me to enter the dream
desde adentro de tu conejito
he wants me inside my rabbit
—with a snap of his fingers
I'm in the watermelon dream

When I get big enough to leave
I forget Chispa and turn my back on
la dulzura del sueño de conejo
the sweetness of the rabbit dream
to live in the other world
in which I drop the watermelon

Paleolithic horse's head carved in low relief
from the cave at Commarque, Dordogne, France.

Source: *Treasures of Prehistoric Art*, by Andre Leroi-Gourham
Henry N. Abrams, Inc. Publishers, New York

A KNOWLEDGE OF WATER

On a caliche cliff overlooking the Rio Grande, my horse Albert
and I watch the sun flash on mica chips in the hills across the
river. Signals pulse from Apache warriors. With a mesquite
stick I draw the skeleton of a fish in the sand. The mouth is
San Antonio, one eye for the ranch in Laredo. The other eye
Nuevo Laredo. The Chihuahuan Desert is the body between
the two Sierras. The tail crosses Monte Alban far to the south.

This desert was once an ocean teeming with fish. I sit
on the edge of its memory feeling the power of the sun.

The faded trail I follow is the way to the next water hole,
not the shortest distance between two points.

Knowledge of water, not a compass, is what one needs
in this desert.

Some fish found in the brackish water of these puddles
dropped from the sky.

WARRIOR HORSE

Bareback like an Apache
I ride my horse Albert
to the top of the caliche cliff
dream I'm the last son of Cochise
all my brothers dead

Cross-legged on a saddle blanket
overlooking the Rio Grande
I pray as the sun reaches its peak
believing I can see all the way to Oaxaca
four hundred miles south

A hole opens in the desert floor
screaming horses with flaming hooves
topple headlong into the tar-rimmed pit
riders float up from their mounts
arms open to the sky

An old Indian told me
this is the place where nothing lives—
a burial ground for old stories
where descendants of the Olmec
lost their Spirit Home

I believe this—
for I saw the sun burn a hole
through the center of the earth
the year before they built the dam
that covers the hole where I buried
my warrior horse

BLUE HORSE

Albert was old when I got him
he might have been a true "blue"
but when I first saw him in the sun
his hide shone through silver
like the skin of a Mexican hairless

On that last day
when his time had come
he led me along caliche cliffs
to a bone drift
at the damp end of a dry creek
where I shot him

I waited
for the buzzards
the maggots and the sun

I waited
for the rainless flood
to tumble-dry his bones

       waited
       for his vowel sounds
       to echo from the cliffs

While I waited
he turned ice-blue
like a fresh-caught trout losing color to the sun

CHILI PIQUINS

Lately, I've been putting cayenne pepper on almost everything I eat. Increasing intensity like an addict. Just last week I bought a package of dried habaneros labeled "hot! 250,000 Scoville units".[6] Trying to think of a recipe, other than for enchiladas or curry, one worthy of such power.

The hottest peppers I knew were chili piquins, about the size of a small pea with a stem. Served uncooked, like jellybeans. Plucked carefully off their stems with the teeth so the juice would not touch your lips. Anywhere the juice touched, outside of the inside of your mouth, would raise a blister. A bite of meat, then two or three chili piquins, then chew holding back the tears. If you cried, you'd cut back on the dose until you built a tolerance.

My father wouldn't touch them. He was from Chicago. My mother, who grew up in Laredo, was a great chili-eater. My brother didn't really try. But, I was the champion. They say capsaicin in chilis brings out endorphins like a runner's high, releasing hormones that turn pain into pleasure.

Our Mexican dog Tigre killed one of my father's guinea hens. To teach the mangy mutt a lesson, my father laced the carcass with ground chilies and forced him to eat it. Later, I found Tigre headlong into the garbage can looking for the rest of his meal. I still eat chili piquins to honor Tigre.

---

6. Scoville Units are named after Wilbur Scoville, a chemist for the Parke Davis pharmaceutical company who, in 1912, invented a method for measuring the heat level of chili peppers. The scale goes from 0 to 15,000,000 for pure capsaicin with the hottest Habaneros at more than 300,000 units. Chili piquins are much hotter than Jalapeños and Cayenne peppers measuring at more than 80,000 Scoville units.

THE BIG "O"

I get anxious when I talk about my father. I remember him as big. Big voice, big chest, big belly. We lived on the Big "O" Ranch. He carried a gun so big it "would stop a Cadillac in its tracks". As a child, he clubbed pigs in the Chicago stockyards. By the time I was born, he and my mother were enemies.

In a picture of my father and mother before they were married, he looks dapper in a dark suit, standing next to his Buick Roadster, one foot on the running board. My mother gazes at him, flapper hat pulled down over bobbed red hair. Her eyes gleam, wet with sex...

A HUNDRED WORDS FOR ANGER

I know its many names
I know when it enters a room
crawling sideways
along yellow papered walls
a frothy slime
oozing from nose-holes of dead fish

I know the way it smells before breakfast
rancid as the hairy armpit
of a harem wife twice betrayed
the sky around it swollen
the color of snow on a tombstone

To the Eskimo
there are a hundred words for snow
for we live and breathe
the elements that surround us
and I was born in a sea of anger

Yes, I know its many faces
I wake up in the morning
looking for it in my bed
I drop from the branch of a tree
and shake out my colors like a giant lizard
until the proper shade of rage unfolds
as I chant the mantra
of the ancient Aztec warrior
    yes, this is a good day to die
    yes, this is a good day to die

Scene of the Dead Man

Paleolithic cave painting.
Lascaux, Dordogne, France

SCENE OF THE DEAD MAN

1.

A wounded bison
guts hanging in loops
Tail raised, head lowered to confront
the stick figure of a man with a hard-on

In his dream the shaman
conjures the kill
so with my father
who took me hunting when I was seven

Drunk, he and his buddies
shout obscenities across the canyon
before I pull their boots off and put them to bed
In the morning, looking at a girlie picture
nailed to the wall, my father says to Johnny Ward
"I still wake up with a hard-on."

Johnny, still half-drunk, takes me for a ride
in his new dark blue souped-up Ford wagon
revving from zero to full speed across an open field
double clutching like a race car driver
lets me off trembling five miles from camp
the day I kill my first buck
gutting it, ladling dark blood from its belly
with cupped hands thinking now I am a man
Fifty years later this morning I wake up
on the cusp of a dream empowered by a hard-on
to write about a cave painting at Lascaux

Before the shaman enters his dream
before the naming and the stories
of Adam, Cain and Abel, of Job,

the toppling of the Tower of Babel
the darkness of the cave was lit
by swirls of energy on stone
carved vulvas, rounded female buttocks
images superimposed
etched over a period of a thousand years
as offerings at a sacred well

2.

This morning I am angry
at my father and the shaman
angry at the power of the dream
the veneration of the erection
the drunk dream, wet dream
stories, the stories
man's tail feathers, iridescent
spread in the darkness of the cave
stealing light
by the ritual wounding of beauty

To the first deer I killed
I say I am sorry, I am ashamed
and from the power of a hard-on
I create my version of the story—
the shaman dies ejaculating
as a man when hanged

I cower at this blasphemy
as Job groveled before Yahweh
My head separates from my body
like the tail of a lizard
growing back but deadened
my body, a living lodestone,
tries to align to true north

but caught in a devil's triangle
spins and wobbles

In this time warp
the shaman does not die
he enters me in the dream
a tapeworm stuck in my gut
feeding gluttonously on fear
growing big as a yellow tree snake

3.

My father stands
in a hospital gown tied in back
the slant of morning sun
burns white around his body
a negative print of Balzac
in a black monk's robe
hands folded across a potbelly
and under his hospital gown
a hard-on

For seven days
my father squares off at death
pacing, trying to find a way out
He rages:
"You'll never make it without me"

Blinded by the glare
I blink at his colossal Olmec head
all jawbone, teeth and forehead
radiant in a last ditch burst
to take everything down with him

I stand my ground in silence
until his power drains away

a puddle of urine under his bed
slithers toward me
a deadly yellow snake without a head

There is a wedge of space
in the shaman's dream
an opening at the moment of killing
before the killing, before dying
before the kingdom of heaven
brought wrack to the sacred heart
where body-mind
merges with the universe

4.

In that sacred space
my body is a jar of fireflies
phosphorescent bones
align with vapor trails in the sky
from last year's migration of geese
beneath my feet
a webbing of ley lines and songlines
connecting earth with body and sky

Unmourned grief
buried deep in stories of land
placenames call to us
cenotaphs by the roadside
pleading to be healed
in the Nahuatl of *Popcatepetl*
Apache of *bizhi igod*
Gaelic of *Poll na gCaorach*
points of alignment
rhymes in a bard's song
y gwir yn erbyn y byd
—truth against the world

5.

I grew up in *Tierra Herida*
wounded borderland
in the lower Rio Grande Valley
where shame flows downriver
a flash flood without rain

As a child I ate tadpole jelly
to become a whale
doused myself with coyote piss
so my humanness wouldn't stink
memorized red and black
letters of the Aztec alphabet
so I could talk with my Nagual

"To Live in the Borderlands means you
are neither *hispana india negra española*
ni gabache, eres mestiza, mulata, half-breed
caught in the crossfire between camps..."
says *una poeta Tejana*[7]

Tengo vergüenza al leer sus palabras
ashamed to read your words
because I was jimmie from laredo
pimply snot nosed kid
nicknamed *zancudo*—sand mosquito
whose father was a big shot
politician, oil man, Texas Ranger
who would shame you
—and I am his son

Ashamed for killing the deer
Tengo vergüenza porque maté el venado

7 *Borderlands, La Frontera* by Gloria Anzaldúa

y porque sé las palabras de la canción
y me quedo en silencio
tengo vergüenza por saber el dolor
y nunca haber vuelto para lamentarlo

La vergüenza está en los cuentos de la tierra
Shame is the story embedded in the land
a scorpion in a boot that stings
when I turn my back to the river
after I shoot my horse and leave home
believing I can forget
who I am and where I come from

6.

I've walked the Comanche Roads
in Zapata County
green roads on the Island of Inishbofin
followed heat seeking butterflies
from Canada to Michoacan
from a mountain of pure crystal
I saw a vision of St Patrick
loud and clear as country western
from XENT radio Mexico
offering 'genuine simulated diamonds'
and 'get your statues of Jesus Christ
it glows in the dark'

Which leaves me with these questions:

If our bones are divining rods
can they find water?

If they were used as pavement
like the bones of butterflies
could our children find their way?

NAMING NAMES

I

Iztacchihautl Popocatepetl
San Juan de Parangarícutiro
San Jose Magote loma de zapote
Xochipilli Xocche Xichu
these words recall the heat
of the Mexican desert in the summer
on the Pan American Highway
between Monterrey and Mexico City
in a 1941 non-airconditioned Cadillac
driving by the sleeping princess *Iztaccihuatl*
and her lover *Popocateptl* kneeling at her side
listening for the first cries of *Paricutin*
their newborn volcano child
erupting from the belly of a corn field
a hundred miles away

II

Forty years later driving through Ireland
looking for my mother's name
in graveyards near the sea
I repeat names of villages in Gaelic
Bun na hAbhann, Lis na nGradh,
Ceann Balor, Macharie Buide
Carraig na Ri

I try to remember the faces
that match the names on the stones
in our Brennan family plot in Laredo
Mike, Susanah, William, Dorothy, Carrie,
Ada, Earlene, Clyde, Maude

I name plants and animals
I knew as a child riding my horse Albert
along the caliche cliffs of the Rio Grande
snakeweed, cholla, creosote, and lechuguilla,
skunks, skinks, javelina, horny toads, rattlers

In the peat bog near Lough Neagh
I go barefoot as I did at the lake in Texas
my toes sink into folds of soggy sphagnum
I say golden gorse, pale purple Erica,
Narthecium, scarlet pimpernel, yellow asphodel

III

In a graveyard near Armagh
in the County of Armagh, when I say
Armagh the name sticks in my throat
knowing this is where people get shot
for being on either side of their fathers
I pray for the 763 victims killed in Armagh
since John Gallagher was shot in 1969

Silently I pray, then out loud say *Mhacha,*
Ard Mhacha, Mhacha of the golden hair
golden *lunulae* and great golden beads
orchards filled with the light of golden apples
ripened on the shores of a lake of golden foam
pissed into life by a giant horse

I think of my father as a child clubbing pigs
in the stockyards of Chicago and I say *muc,*
Muckelty Muckish Muckery Mucshnamh
"a place where pigs swim across the little lake"
I think of Portmuck at Islandmagee

where I studied poetry one lovely summer
with Jimmie Simmons and wonder if I should
dig up my father's body and re-bury it
here in the mystical land of *Emmania Mhacha*

IV

Iztaccihuatl Popocatepetl
San Juan de Parangaricutiro
San Jose Magote loma del zapote
Xochipilli Xocche Xichu
these words spoken in prayer
to return the breath of each name
into the mouth of its headstone
and on the lap of my mother's grave
as an infant were-jaguar
seeking protection of the fire god *Xictli*
as *mariposas* seek the volcano
to find their way home each year
in the mountains of Michoacan
on *el Día de los Muertos*

THE SEARCH

Clonmacnois
Ancient monastic site, Co. Offaly, Ireland

AT MY MOTHER'S GRAVE

I wait for stones to break the silence. And so my journey begins, looking for the perfect stone: marble in the Aran Islands, quartz at Crough Patrick, obsidian at the pyramid of Xictli in the Pedregal. I follow migrations of butterflies and whales to learn their secret. On hands and knees I re-enter the womb of earth beneath the mound at Newgrange. I take a stone from the great wall of *Dun Aonghasa,* have it cut to a high-cross and inscribed with a Gaelic prayer for my mother.

The colors of earth are drained by the desert sun
leaving each day silent.

I taste a pinch of earth from my mother's grave
recalling the smell of tidal pools and oyster beds.

An ancient glacier breaks the silence with the moan
of a cow giving birth.

STONEMASON

My stonemason John says
he uses Elberton granite from Georgia
It has the best grain and lasts the longest
How long is long I ask
Oh he says a thousand years

I want more than hard gray stone
to guard her silence
I want stone that stays alive
a megalith jammed deep into earth
an antenna to amplify the signals
emitted from her ash and bone

I went to Ireland
looking for the perfect stone
found stone cottages and monuments
mountains and fields of stone
continuous rows of stonewalls
wound round the island like an offering

I found stone carvings of mermaids
and ancient unnamed river gods
a Sheela-na-Gig I thought I recognized
having seen her name
on the walls of a cave in the Dordogne
along with her portrait cut and shaped
on the rounded surface of soft white stone

There are no stones
where my mother and I were born
only the jagged edges of memory
ground down by the desert *molcajete*[8]

8. Kitchen mortar made of volcanic rock

to caliche and polished round pebbles
leaving no trace of history
but an abandoned *pulque* farm
an adobe jail
and a dried-up river bed

HONORING THE STONES

1

In the Brennan family plot
I take off my jacket
shirt sticking to my body
remembering how I turned away
from Brennan kisses
ashamed in the presence of my father
Shuffling, I look down at my feet
not knowing what to say to the stones

I remember—
my mother combs her red hair
after giving me a bath
a photo of grandpa Brennan
in his County Sheriff's uniform
Aunt Ada, who married a Mexican
brags he was pure-blooded *Toltec*
My father's voice drowns them out
like a flash flood in the desert

My heart whirrs like a frightened rabbit
I transfer her ashes
from a plastic urn to a *Cántaro.*
Her body purified by fire
pours hot through my fingers
reminding me she wanted the last word—
not to be buried next to him

More than forty years ago
after my father's funeral
my mother and I returned to the ranch

lit a bonfire, took down his pictures
Holding hands in silence
we watched the embers burn down

2

In search of the perfect stone
I go to Clonmacnois
kneel at the Cross of the Scriptures
and say a prayer for King Flann
son of Maelsechnaill and for Colman
the stonemason who made the cross

At the Nun's Chapel
I pray to the goddess Brigid
sainted Sheela-na-Gig
who glares down from the portal
exposed pudenda
to remind us of where we came from

I follow ancient tracks
of *Tuatha De Danann*
who descended into earth
through fairy mounds
at *Tara* and *Emain Macha*
and at Newgrange
the procession of *Ban Fis*
when Dagda the Sun God
penetrates the womb of earth

I crawl into the tombs
of Loughcrew and Carrowkeel
At Carrowmore I feel the heat
of a "soul egg" in my hand

—a polished white stone
charged with the breath of a beloved
waiting to be released

3

As I place the perfect stone
on my mother's grave
I think of my father
of blue skies and black bullwhips

how we hold to our fathers
through earth and fire
and the smell of bones

hold to our mothers
by the taste of earth
and the permanence of stone

THE MILL HAG

How beautiful she must have been
before she posed as Venus of Laussel
her face seen as swirls of light
essence beyond the profanity of body

Her name chiseled on cave walls
to the soft sounds of the word vulva
repeated as a Chinese calligrapher
might practice his ancient art

How beautiful she was as Tiamet
before she was betrayed by Marduk
before she became the white bull goddess
and crossed the sea on a wave of fury

Before being cursed and betrayed
before she abandoned her own son
and cast the testicles of her seed-bull lover
into the lake at Navan

Before being hacked up
parts strewn to the four corners of earth
bones burnt and buried
under mounds of granite and greywacke

No tomb strong enough to hold her
she emerges with the tide
a demon rising from the sea
she reappears as vulture goddess
vagina exposed as our beloved
Sidhe Sile Sheela-na-Gig

Transformed into the Mill Hag
she chases Mad Sweeney
across the Muckish mountains
crashing into the cliff at Dunseverick

At the Nun's Chapel at Clonmacnois
her naked bird-frame body
glares down at me from above the doorway
legs spread wrapped around her head
and dragged from her rafter in Killua
a screeching plucked wet hawk
with a beak between her legs

When I found her hooded and chained
on a white pedestal behind an open door
I wanted to tuck her inside my shirt
and press her against the warmth of my belly

I think of my mother's rage
when I buried her charred remains
beside her tormentor
a ninety nine year old goddess
transformed by age and fire

Sesskilgrene
Standing stone. Sesskilgrene, Co. Tyrone, Ireland

Source: *Megalithic Art in Ireland*, Muiris O'Sullivan

SESSKILGRENE

Where is Sesskilgrene?
You're standing in it he says
while pumping gas
I mean the sacred stone

Oh, ay he says—
take the road back there
(a sweep of the hand)
past the second farm house

which may not be occupied
since Hackett's brother died last fall
go behind the barn
through the gate on the right

to the second field there
another gate
up on the hill in the middle
...you can't miss it

A single standing stone
unattended
but for a circle of cows
staring as if I have no right

I kneel before the grave
into damp earth
trace faded swirls and dots
with charged fingers

barely touch an eye
seeing a face
pocked with black lichen
perhaps the portrait of a goddess

top half rubbed smooth
from cows scratching their bums
I reach out to the cold stone
embracing her cries

THE TRIPLE GODDESS

Spirals on a stone placed upright half in half out
of the ground. Her vulva opens to embrace the seed
planted in her belly by the phallus beam of the sun.

Her body resonates with infusion of light,
expands in waves until she explodes in a ball of fire
leaving stretch-marks across the belly of sky.

She transforms from maiden to crone
passing through her mother phase in song.
Her music fades as we forget the words...

clouds turn into anvils and thunderheads,
forge the fear we use against the hag.
We chase her into the cliffs at Ailsa Craig

where her bones lie bleaching on rocks
until Brigid, sainted goddess of the sun,
appears at Mary's side, with three drops

from the holy well at Cill-Dare,
sprinkled on the head of the child Jesus,
converts the triple goddess to the Trinity.

At Candlemas, the wail of the Uillean Pipe
mourns the loss of words to her song—
Brigid's snake spirals back into its mound

and a finger rubs the vulva of the Sheela-na-Gig
quickening the womb of Death made fertile
as I place this stone on my mother's grave.

THE RUIN

The sun god, the goddess of the moon and the dark goddess of the crossways lived in an age before fire and ice. Before the first stone was planted in the sea off the coast of Donegal. First the stone and then the word. The word and then the stories. In the stories the sun god penetrates the womb of earth on a ramp of stone. Kings issue from caves and the light of the moon goddess is eternally eclipsed by the sun. Each kingdom lost to the sea.

Darwin stood on the edge of time and told what he saw. When I think of Darwin I think of Job. Both dared speak out in the face of God. I knew this truth in my father's rage but could not speak. The silence returns when I stand before the broken walls of a temple.

A ruin is a holograph of the history of man. What is hidden is known by the body.

The gap between the first word and the history of earth is a wound of silence.

First came the word, but the power of a word is in the silence that precedes it.

UNMARKED GRAVES

The earth grows heavy going west
green surrenders to bogs and rocks
clachans—tiny stone villages
abandoned, fallen into ruins
the *Burren* a mountain of stone
adds weight to the land
its massive form echoed at sea
in the gray limestone body of Aran

On the island of Innishmore
inside the great circle of stone
I drop to all fours
crawl to the edge of the cliff
look straight down
where the flat slab of earth breaks off
taking the dream of Dun Aonghosa
into the sea along with the wall

I hear prayers rendered in stone
walls linking father to son
mountains stripped of green
leaving bones of history
poking through worn-out earth—
rubbled walls
in as many shapes as Irish words
for the sound of scattered stone
cloch, clochar, clochrach,

> *Le allas a bhaithis*
> *Le fuil a chroi*
> *Deanfaidh se talamh*
> *As na scalprachai*[9]

"With the sweat of his brow
with the blood of his heart
he will make land
out of the stone."

9. From a poem by Tomas O. Direan.
Scalprechai—a green field reclaimed from bare rock by
spreading sand and seaweed.

CEIDE FIELDS

A rainy August on a hillside above Ceide
the Atlantic catches light in long rhomboid streaks moving
left to right across its smooth metal surface

The sun breaks through layers of low-hanging clouds
illuminating first one field then another across the valley
hovering above one bright small square in the patchwork

walls of buried fields light up green like foot bones
seen through the lens of a shoe store fluoroscope
5000 years of history mummy-wrapped in a bog

A passing cloud of rain merges midair with the sea
on shore it licks placenta of flesh and bone
collapsing light-years as in myth or the study of stars

In my dream I approach shore standing in the prow
of the small wooden skiff unsteady as we land
greeted by men in sandals and black robes

Holy men who would explain my father to me
but I do not want to hear them
I want to walk up the mountain with bare feet

a *castrato* leaving a trail of bloody footprints
to fling my manhood into a stranger's doorway
anger appeased by killing my father's seed

but on this hillside I choke on charged air
yearning to fall between the cracks of time
to re-enter that moment of grace

when my father's fathers built the first field
stone by stone a monument of 2500 acres
reaching as newborn earth to meet the sky

not knowing what went wrong nor what got lost
between the first farm and the last potato
between Ireland and Laredo

the wound of my father's barbed wire fences
stretched piano wire tight across Texas desert
one more crude stitching of that festered wound

Burial place at Creac'h Quille, At the entryway, a stele carved
with a pair of breasts and a necklace.

District of Saint Quai-Perros, Cotes d'Amor, France

CREAC'H QUILLE

On the coast of St. Quay-Perros, the stones turn from gray to red. At dusk, the sun spreads a blush across the tomb of the goddess-mother. Her children are gone, they've forgotten her. Even their bones have washed away.

    I feel shame
    as I come upon the goddess
    carved on the facing stone

    dog turd at the entryway
    temple stones unearthed
    its covering mound worn away

    she is naked
    breasts and necklace
    waiting to be addressed

WHAT TO SAY TO THE STONES

1.

After my mother's funeral, I walk among the twenty three graves in the family plot writing down names and dates. I try to remember the stories, to recall a face, a voice, but they are gone. The buzz of the cicadas grows louder. I touch my grandfather's stone to feel a vibration, a connection. Nothing. I take a pinch of fresh earth from my mother's grave and eat it.

The sun burns a hole through the yellow sky from the Mexican side of the river. I smell my childhood and shrink into my knees like dismounting at the end of a day's ride. I remember the bone drift in the dry creek where I buried my horse Albert. At night, the bones had eyes and danced.

> Jacob believed his stone pillow was holy because of a dream. His pillow became the cornerstone of the House of God.

> In England, a Thunderstone is placed under the throne of the King.

> In Ireland, a stone is kept in the house to talk to when a loved one dies.

> Under my bed, I keep a picture of my mother and a pair of old boots I wore when I rode.

2.

My mother let me touch the birthing scar I made, a four inch welt across her belly. Before I could talk, I made a vow to her but she never told me what it was. At her grave, when I touched her stone, I felt a burning on my cheek.

Now, I bow to enter the tumulus of Gavrinis. Twenty six engraved pillar-stones line the walls in a profusion of swirls. The dark passageway is an incision in the belly of earth.

The next morning
I start to write something
I think I understand about stone

at that moment
a blue bowl in the cupboard
explodes

3.

The goddess materializes from fragments of memory. Dots, circles, vulva, the squatting body of a Venus giving birth, wasp-waist goddess with ringlet curls. She explodes into shards, her energy transforms into menacing clouds of black rain. I stand silent before her rage—

I recognize the voice of the goddess,
a string of human hearts around her throat.

I knew her when she had a herd of black goats
and danced with snakes.

When it rained, I caught water moccasins
and delivered them to her in a gunny sack.

She speaks of penalties for broken contracts
between absorber and emitter,

agreements sealed by mutual vibration,
as between a magnolia blossom and a bat.

4.

Near the sea, in the tumulus of Pierre Plates, I trace engravings
on a pillar stone with a flashlight. Curves, meanders, a tablet
of instructions. A labyrinth, a maze, a map for the journey to
the next world. My footprints appear on the wall as I take a
breath. The stones come alive as a song. Do I need to know
the words?

> The path is traced in the sand
> the goddess erases half of it
> requiring me to remember
> the steps of the dance
>
> Am I the bull-leaper
> who defies the Minotaur
> the Hopi deer dancer
> who eats the heart of his prey?

5.

At Carnac I follow a mile long alignment of megaliths feeling the weight of stones as they increase in size. At the top of the hill, I stand uneasy before the circle of stones. Nothing between them and bare earth, the altar open to the sky.

> The earth fiery beneath my feet
> as it pushes up to meet the sky

> Are these the Olmec gods I knew as a child?
> Does my grandfather Brennan stand trial here?

> I learned when to twist the yellow gourd from its vine
> to preserve the sweetness

> How a desert holds the fragrance of a flower
> and guards its seed for 100 dry years.

THE MONARCHS

On the day of the dead
mariposas return
to the mountains of Michoacan
orange wings
beating to the rhythm of fire
a great procession
Tibetan Monks in saffron robes
winding from tree-tops into the sun

In the sanctuary of El Rosario
a canopy of low-hanging clouds
draped with a blazing tapestry
woven in full flight
our earth-bound spell
led by butterflies
these spirits of the dead
leave a carpet of broken wings
strewn at our feet like petals

Before Conquistadores named the land
before mapping the Camino Real
monarchs built their own royal road
from the ice fields of Canada
south 2000 miles
to the valley of the fire gods
paved with the wings and dust
of their dead

And for 100 generations
of the millions that followed
not even one has yet made the journey
from beginning to end

LAS MARIPOSAS

En el día de los muertos
regresan las mariposas
a las montañas de Michoacán
alas anaranjadas
laten al ritmo de fuego
una gran procesión
de monjes Tibetanos en tunicas de azafran
serpenteando las copas de los árboles
hacia el sol

En el refugio sagrado del Rosario
una bóveda de nubes bajas
cubierta con tapiz flamante
tejido en pleno vuelo
nuestro encuentro terrenal
guiado por estas mariposas
almas de muertos
que dejan alfombra de alas quebradas
echada como flores en las senda

Antes que los conquistadores
nombraran la tierra
antes que trazaran el Camino Real
los monarcas fundaron su propia vía regia
de los campos helados de Canadá
dos mil millas al sur hasta el valle
de los dioses de fuego
lo pavimentaron con alas y polvo
de sus muertos

Y por un sinnúmero de años
de los millones que lo siguieron
aún ninguno ha hecho el viaje
del principio al fin

O'HERN

Fan, a thaistealai
agus cuir paidir
le hanamacha
mo mhuintire

Say a prayer for my "Muddy"
Sue Brennan O'Hern

JAMES O'HERN grew up on a ranch in Laredo, Texas. He attended Kemper Military School in Missouri, Southern Methodist University in Texas, and the New York University Graduate School of Business in New York. For more than thirty years, he has been an investment banker and corporate executive in New York, London, and Los Angeles. Currently, he resides in New York City.

The two great influences on him as a youth were his mother, Sue Brennan O'Hern, and a Mestizo ranch hand, Chispa. His mother impressed upon him the importance of seeking his roots, of "finding out who you are and where you come from." After her death, he went to Ireland to find the perfect stone for her and stayed on, taking a course in Ancient Irish Archeology and visiting holy sites all across Ireland, and thus begun his world-wide tour of holy sites to seek a vision of unity and a connection with the ancient past. Mentored as a child by Chispa, O'Hern absorbed Chispa's native culture, including its deep respect for nature and its visionary character. Chispa in some ways became his spiritual father, initiating him into native lore and the ancient customs of the Southwest. The influence of these two people helped him reject the racist and violent culture of his Texan father and prepared him for the search that was to come.

Later, he was also deeply affected by the works of Joy Harjo and Gloria Anzaldua, and through his mediations and his travels to sacred sites, continued to seek a vision of unity and spiritual connection. "If you are true to that seeking," he says, "you go wherever it takes you. There are no borders." Everywhere he traveled physically or mentally, he found images at sacred sites that validated a primal vision of unity between man and the natural world, as well as a reverence for life—a vision that was often lost, neglected or scorned as Western society "developed."

"What I'm trying to do," O'Hern comments, "is to bring a new perspective to things that have been buried"

CURBSTONE PRESS, INC.

is a non-profit publishing house dedicated to literature that reflects a
commitment to social change, with an emphasis on contemporary writing
from Latino, Latin American and Vietnamese cultures. Curbstone presents
writers who give voice to the unheard in a language that goes beyond
denunciation to celebrate, honor and teach. Curbstone builds bridges
between its writers and the public – from inner-city to rural areas, colleges to
community centers, children to adults. Curbstone seeks out the highest
aesthetic expression of the dedication to human rights and intercultural
understanding: poetry, testimonies, novels, stories,
and children's books.

This mission requires more than just producing books. It requires ensuring
that as many people as possible learn about these books and read them. To
achieve this, a large portion of Curbstone's schedule is dedicated to
arranging tours and programs for its authors, working with public school
and university teachers to enrich curricula, reaching out to underserved
audiences by donating books and conducting readings and community
programs, and promoting discussion in the media. It is only through these
combined efforts that literature can truly make a difference.

Curbstone Press, like all non-profit presses, depends on the support of
individuals, foundations, and government agencies to bring you, the reader,
works of literary merit and social significance which might not find a place
in profit-driven publishing channels, and to bring the authors and their
books into communities across the country. Our sincere thanks to the many
individuals, foundations, and government agencies who have recently
supported this endeavor: Connecticut Commission on the Arts, Connecticut
Humanities Council, Fisher Foundation, Greater Hartford Arts Council,
Hartford Courant Foundation, J. M. Kaplan Fund, Lannan Foundation, John
D. and Catherine T. MacArthur Foundation, National Endowment for the
Arts, Open Society Institute, Puffin Foundation, and the Woodrow Wilson
National Fellowship Foundation.

Please help to support Curbstone's efforts to present the diverse voices and
views that make our culture richer. Tax-deductible donations can be made
by check or credit card to:
Curbstone Press, 321 Jackson Street, Willimantic, CT 06226
phone: (860) 423-5110   fax: (860) 423-9242
www.curbstone.org

IF YOU WOULD LIKE TO BE A MAJOR SPONSOR OF A
CURBSTONE BOOK, PLEASE CONTACT US.